NATURE WATCH

WHALES AND DOLPHINS

Robin Kerrod

Consultant: Michael Bright

LORENZ BOOKS

This edition is published by Hermes House
an imprint of Anness Publishing Ltd
Hermes House, 88–89 Blackfriars Road, London SE1 8HA
tel. 020 7401 2077; fax 020 7633 9499

www.hermeshouse.com; www.annesspublishing.com

If you like the images in this book and
would like to investigate using them
for publishing, promotions or
advertising, please visit our website
www.practicalpictures.com for
more information.

Publisher: Joanna Lorenz
Managing Editor, Children's Books:
Linda Fraser
Senior Editor: Nicole Pearson
Editor: Louisa Somerville
Designer: Vivienne Gordon
Illustration: Julian Baker, David Webb

ETHICAL TRADING POLICY
Because of our ongoing ecological investment
programme, you, as our customer, can have the
pleasure and reassurance of knowing that a tree is
being cultivated on your behalf to naturally replace the
materials used to make the book you are holding.
For further information about this scheme, go to
www.annesspublishing.com/trees

PICTURE CREDITS
b=bottom, t=top, c=centre, l=left, r=right
Animals Animals: pages 11tr, 38tc, 45c and 55t; Bruce
Coleman: pages 4b, 9b, 13tr, 13br, 15tl, 19tl, 20t, 21t,
22t, 27b, 39t, 42b, 43c, 45t, 46t, 48b, 54b, 57t, 60t,
61c and cover; Bridgeman Art Library: pages 31cr and
59b; Ecoscene: pages 8cb, 8bl, 9c and 41br; Mary
Evans Picture Library: page 9tl; FLPA: pages 2, 3, 7tr,
7bl, 10t, 10bl, 12b, 14t, 19cl, 19cr, 23t, 24c, 30c, 32-
33, 32t, 32b, 34b, 35t, 36-37, 36l, 42t, 50t, 50bl, 52-
53, 52cl, 52b, 53bl, 54c, 55b, 56t, 58b, 61t, cover and
title page; NASA: page 17br; Natural History Museum:
pages 4-5c, 6c and 49cl; Natural Science Photos: pages
18c and 26b; Nature Photographers: pages 11c and
58t; NHPA: pages 12tr, 15b, 24tl, 24b, 29t, 29b, 34t,
35b, 37t, 37b, 38bl, 56c, 57c, 57b, 58c and 61b;
Oxford Scientific Films: pages 2, 5bl, 6b, 8cr, 13bl,
16bl, 16br, 18tl, 20b, 21b, 22c, 22b, 25b, 27b, 28t,
28b, 29cl, 29cr, 30b, 31t, 31cl, 33b, 35c, 36b, 38cr,
39b, 40b, 41t, 41bl, 42c, 43t, 44c, 49cr, 49b, 55c, 56b,
59t, cover and title page; Planet Earth Pictures: pages
2, 4tr, 11bl, 14b, 16t, 18b, 19b, 23c, 25t, 26, 30t, 31b,
39c, 44t, 44b, 45b, 46c, 46b, 47t, 47c, 47b, 48t, 49t,
50c, 51cr, 51bl, 51br, 53cr, 54t, 59c, 60b and cover;
Spacecharts: page 5tl and 17b; Visual Arts Library:
pages 10cr, 15c and 53br; Zefa Pictures: pages 5tr and
51t.

C O N T E N T S

TENTS

WHALE ORDER

Whales and dolphins are among the most delightful creatures on Earth. Like fish, they spend all their lives in the sea and are masters of their watery habitat. But unlike fish, they breathe air, have warm blood and suckle their young. They are more closely related to human beings than fish because they are mammals. Many whales are enormous – some are as big and as heavy as a railway carriage full of passengers. Dolphins are much smaller – most are about the same size as an adult human being. Porpoises, which look much like dolphins, are also roughly the same size as humans.

Although they are much smaller, dolphins and porpoises are in fact kinds of whales, too. All whales, large and small, belong to the major group, or order, of animals called Cetacea. The word comes from the Greek word cetus, meaning sea monster. From the word Cetacea comes the word cetacean, which means any kind of whale.

humpback whale

HEAVYWEIGHTS

The largest of the whales are the biggest animals that have ever lived on Earth. This leaping humpback whale is nearly 15m long and weighs over 25 tonnes – as much as five fully-grown elephants. Some other kinds of whales, such as the fin and blue whales, are very much bigger than this.

WHALE ANCESTORS

More than 50 million years ago, creatures like this were swimming in the seas. They seem to have been ancestors of modern cetaceans. This creature, named basilosaurus (meaning king lizard), grew up to over 20m long. It had a snake-like body with tiny front flippers and traces of a pair of hind limbs.

BALEEN WHALES

These humpback whales are feeding in Alaskan waters. They belong to the group, or suborder, of whales known as the baleen whales. The baleen, or whalebone, whales are in general very much larger than those in the other main group, the toothed whales. Although the baleen whales include the largest animals on Earth, they feed on some of the very smallest.

humpback whales

WHALE IN THE SKY

This star map shows a constellation of stars named Cetus, meaning the sea monster or whale. In Greek mythology, Cetus was a monster that was about to devour Andromeda, a beautiful maiden who had been chained to a rock as a sacrifice. Along came the hero Perseus, who killed the sea monster and saved Andromeda.

basilosaurus

bottlenose dolphin

TOOTHED WHALES

A bottlenose dolphin opens its mouth and shows its teeth. It is one of the many species of toothed whales. Toothed whales have much simpler teeth than land mammals and many more of them. The bottlenose dolphin, for example, has up to 50 teeth in both its upper and lower jaws.

AIR BREATHERS

Because they are mammals, all whales and dolphins breathe air. Here, a common dolphin is breathing out through a blowhole on top of its head as it rises to the surface. These dolphins usually breathe several times a minute, although they can hold their breath for five minutes or more when diving.

common dolphin

Did you know? A blue whale can weigh as much as 25 elephants.

WHALES LARGE AND SMALL

The word whale conjures up a picture of a huge creature – and some whales really are vast. Most of the biggest ones belong to the major group of cetaceans called the baleen whales. These whales do not have teeth in their mouth. Instead they have brush-like plates, called baleen, that hang from their upper jaw. They use the baleen to filter their food from the water. One large whale that does not belong to the baleen group is the sperm whale. It has teeth, not baleen, and belongs to the other major cetacean group, called the toothed whales. This group also includes the much smaller dolphins, porpoises, white whales and beaked whales. All these cetaceans have teeth for biting and grasping the prey they feed on.

grey whale

GREY WHALE

The massive grey whale can grow up to nearly 15m long, and tip the scales at 35 tonnes or more. It is a similar size to the humpback, sei, bowhead and right whales, but is quite different in appearance. Instead of the smooth skin of the other whales, the grey has rough skin and no proper dorsal fin on its back.

Did you know? Some whales have as many as 3,000 baleen plates in their jaws.

beluga and bowhead whales

BOWHEAD AND BELUGA

At 16m the bowhead whale, which has a highly curved jaw, can grow as large as the sei whale. It is closely related to the right whale, which can be slightly bigger, at 18m. The bowhead is famous for its long baleen plates and extremely thick layer of blubber. The toothed whales we call belugas *(above left)* never grow longer than about 5m. The first part of the word beluga means white in Russian and belugas are also commonly known as white whales.

SEI WHALE

At up to about 16m, the sei whale can grow slightly longer than the grey. It looks much like its bigger relatives, the blue whale and the fin. They are all members of the group called rorquals, which have deep grooves in their throat. These grooves allow the throat to expand greatly when the animals take great mouthfuls of water for feeding. A sei whale has up to 60 grooves in its throat, while a fin whale has up to 100.

sei whale

Did you know? The blue whale's tongue weighs as much as an African elephant.

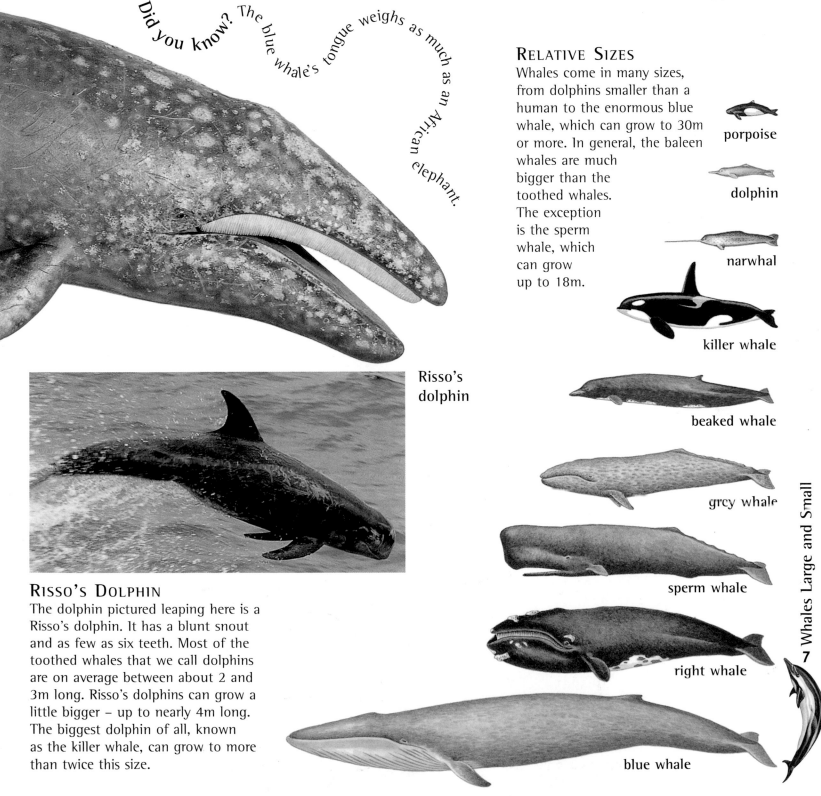

Risso's dolphin

RELATIVE SIZES

Whales come in many sizes, from dolphins smaller than a human to the enormous blue whale, which can grow to 30m or more. In general, the baleen whales are much bigger than the toothed whales. The exception is the sperm whale, which can grow up to 18m.

porpoise

dolphin

narwhal

killer whale

beaked whale

grey whale

sperm whale

right whale

blue whale

RISSO'S DOLPHIN

The dolphin pictured leaping here is a Risso's dolphin. It has a blunt snout and as few as six teeth. Most of the toothed whales that we call dolphins are on average between about 2 and 3m long. Risso's dolphins can grow a little bigger – up to nearly 4m long. The biggest dolphin of all, known as the killer whale, can grow to more than twice this size.

WHALE BONES

Like all mammals, whales have a skeleton of bones. The skeleton helps give the body its shape and also protects vital organs like the heart. Unlike land mammals, a whale's body is supported by the surrounding water. For this reason, the bones of whales are not as strong as those of land mammals, and are quite soft and spongy. The main part of the whale skeleton is the long backbone, made up of many vertebrae. Joints between the vertebrae give the backbone some flexibility. The backbone provides some body support. However, it acts mainly as a strong anchor for the whale's muscles, particularly the powerful swimming muscles that drive the tail. Instead of a land mammal's limbs, a whale has a pair of modified fore limbs, called flippers. It uses the flippers as paddles for manoeuvring in the water.

WHALEBONE CORSET

This is an advertisement for a whalebone corset. It dates from 1911. Corsets were once worn by women to give them a shapely figure. The corsets, in fact, were not made of the bones of whales, but the baleen plates found in the mouths of the baleen whales. The plates were misnamed whalebones.

UNDERNEATH THE ARCHES

Arches built from the jaw bones of huge baleen whales can be seen in some ports that were once the home of whaling fleets. This example of a jaw bone arch can be seen in Port Stanley in the Falkland Islands. It is located outside Christ Church Cathedral. Nowadays, whales are protected species. Building such arches is now forbidden.

HANDS UP

The bones in a sperm whale's flipper are remarkably similar to those in a human hand. A whale's flippers are a much changed version of a typical mammal's front limbs. Both hands have wrist bones, finger bones and joints.

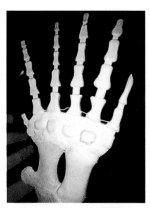

sperm whale flipper

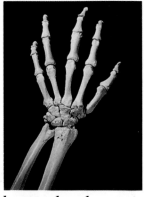

human hand

WHALE BONES

Like all mammals, whales have a skeleton of bones. The skeleton helps give the body its shape and also protects vital organs like the heart. Unlike land mammals, a whale's body is supported by the surrounding water. For this reason, the bones of whales are not as strong as those of land mammals, and are quite soft and spongy. The main part of the whale skeleton is the long backbone, made up of many vertebrae. Joints between the vertebrae give the backbone some flexibility. The backbone provides some body support. However, it acts mainly as a strong anchor for the whale's muscles, particularly the powerful swimming muscles that drive the tail. Instead of a land mammal's limbs, a whale has a pair of modified fore limbs, called flippers. It uses the flippers as paddles for manoeuvring in the water.

WHALEBONE CORSET
This is an advertisement for a whalebone corset. It dates from 1911. Corsets were once worn by women to give them a shapely figure. The corsets, in fact, were not made of the bones of whales, but the baleen plates found in the mouths of the baleen whales. The plates were misnamed whalebones.

UNDERNEATH THE ARCHES
Arches built from the jaw bones of huge baleen whales can be seen in some ports that were once the home of whaling fleets. This example of a jaw bone arch can be seen in Port Stanley in the Falkland Islands. It is located outside Christ Church Cathedral. Nowadays, whales are protected species. Building such arches is now forbidden.

HANDS UP
The bones in a sperm whale's flipper are remarkably similar to those in a human hand. A whale's flippers are a much changed version of a typical mammal's front limbs. Both hands have wrist bones, finger bones and joints.

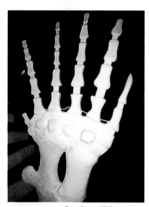

sperm whale flipper

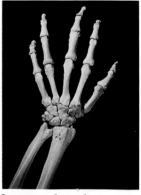

human hand

SEI WHALE

At up to about 16m, the sei whale can grow slightly longer than the grey. It looks much like its bigger relatives, the blue whale and the fin. They are all members of the group called rorquals, which have deep grooves in their throat. These grooves allow the throat to expand greatly when the animals take great mouthfuls of water for feeding. A sei whale has up to 60 grooves in its throat, while a fin whale has up to 100.

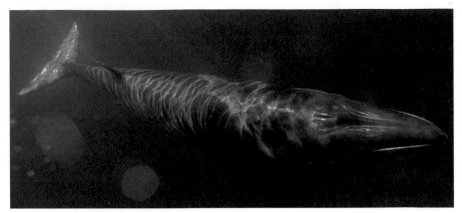

sei whale

Did you know? The blue whale's tongue weighs as much as an African elephant.

RELATIVE SIZES

Whales come in many sizes, from dolphins smaller than a human to the enormous blue whale, which can grow to 30m or more. In general, the baleen whales are much bigger than the toothed whales. The exception is the sperm whale, which can grow up to 18m.

Risso's dolphin

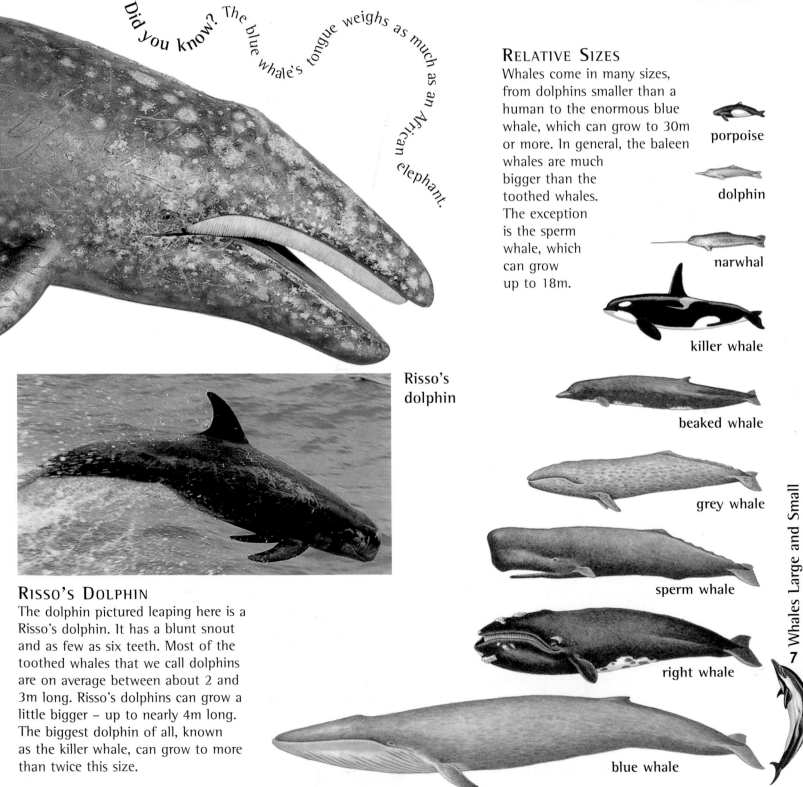

porpoise

dolphin

narwhal

killer whale

beaked whale

grey whale

sperm whale

right whale

blue whale

RISSO'S DOLPHIN

The dolphin pictured leaping here is a Risso's dolphin. It has a blunt snout and as few as six teeth. Most of the toothed whales that we call dolphins are on average between about 2 and 3m long. Risso's dolphins can grow a little bigger – up to nearly 4m long. The biggest dolphin of all, known as the killer whale, can grow to more than twice this size.

WHALES LARGE AND SMALL

The word whale conjures up a picture of a huge creature – and some whales really are vast. Most of the biggest ones belong to the major group of cetaceans called the baleen whales. These whales do not have teeth in their mouth. Instead they have brush-like plates, called baleen, that hang from their upper jaw. They use the baleen to filter their food from the water. One large whale that does not belong to the baleen group is the sperm whale. It has teeth, not baleen, and belongs to the other major cetacean group, called the toothed whales. This group also includes the much smaller dolphins, porpoises, white whales and beaked whales. All these cetaceans have teeth for biting and grasping the prey they feed on.

grey whale

GREY WHALE
The massive grey whale can grow up to nearly 15m long, and tip the scales at 35 tonnes or more. It is a similar size to the humpback, sei, bowhead and right whales, but is quite different in appearance. Instead of the smooth skin of the other whales, the grey has rough skin and no proper dorsal fin on its back.

Did you know? Some whales have as many as 3,000 baleen plates in their jaws.

beluga and
bowhead whales

BOWHEAD AND BELUGA
At 16m the bowhead whale, which has a highly curved jaw, can grow as large as the sei whale. It is closely related to the right whale, which can be slightly bigger, at 18m. The bowhead is famous for its long baleen plates and extremely thick layer of blubber. The toothed whales we call belugas (above left) never grow longer than about 5m. The first part of the word beluga means white in Russian and belugas are also commonly known as white whales.

WHALE IN THE SKY

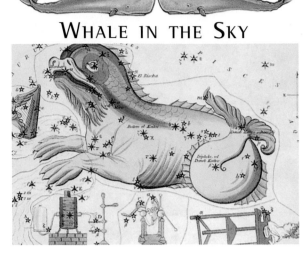

This star map shows a constellation of stars named Cetus, meaning the sea monster or whale. In Greek mythology, Cetus was a monster that was about to devour Andromeda, a beautiful maiden who had been chained to a rock as a sacrifice. Along came the hero Perseus, who killed the sea monster and saved Andromeda.

bottlenose dolphin

basilosaurus

TOOTHED WHALES
A bottlenose dolphin opens its mouth and shows its teeth. It is one of the many species of toothed whales. Toothed whales have much simpler teeth than land mammals and many more of them. The bottlenose dolphin, for example, has up to 50 teeth in both its upper and lower jaws.

AIR BREATHERS
Because they are mammals, all whales and dolphins breathe air. Here, a common dolphin is breathing out through a blowhole on top of its head as it rises to the surface. These dolphins usually breathe several times a minute, although they can hold their breath for five minutes or more when diving.

common dolphin

Did you know? A blue whale can weigh as much as 25 elephants.

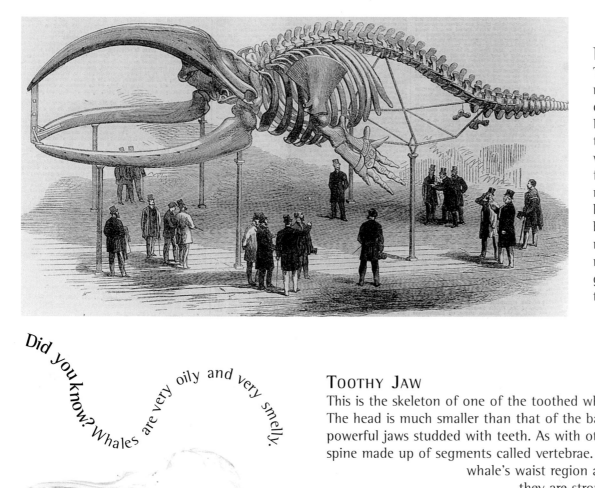

BIG HEAD
This huge skeleton of a right whale was put on display in London in 1830. Its large jaw bones tell us that it is a baleen whale, which needs a big mouth for feeding. As with other mammals, the whale has a large rib cage to protect its body organs. Unlike land mammals, however, it has no hind limbs or pelvic girdle – just a few tiny bones.

Did you know? Whales are very oily and very smelly.

TOOTHY JAW
This is the skeleton of one of the toothed whales, the false killer whale. The head is much smaller than that of the baleen whales, and it has powerful jaws studded with teeth. As with other whales, it has a long spine made up of segments called vertebrae. The vertebrae in the whale's waist region are large. This is so that they are strong enough to anchor the animal's powerful tail muscles.

false killer whale skeleton

KILLER SKULL
This skull of a killer whale was found on the seashore. Both the upper and lower jaws are studded with vicious teeth, which curve inwards and backwards. The teeth are more than 10cm long. When it was alive, the whale would have been a deadly predator, attacking seals, dolphins and sometimes whales that were even bigger than itself.

killer whale skull

WHALE BODIES

On the outside, whales could hardly be more different from land mammals. Over many millions of years they have developed quite distinct features that suit them to a life spent mostly underwater. They have long, rounded bodies and smooth, almost hairless, skin. Like fish, whales move about using fins. They have a large head and a very short neck, which most species cannot move. On the inside, whales are similar to land mammals. They have the same body organs, such as heart, lungs, stomach, intestines, kidneys and sex organs. The main difference is that in the big whales, the body organs are much larger than in land mammals.

bottlenose dolphins

BIG MOUTH

A grey whale surfaces, mouth wide open, to look around. It is one of the baleen whales, and the baleen can be seen hanging from its upper jaw. Baleen whales need a big mouth so that they can take in large mouthfuls of water when they are feeding. Grey whales usually feed at the bottom of the sea.

baleen

grey whale

JONAH AND THE WHALE

This picture from the 17th century tells one of the best known of all Bible stories. The prophet Jonah was thrown overboard by sailors during a terrible storm. To rescue him, God sent a whale, which swallowed him whole. Jonah spent three days in the whale's belly before it coughed him up on to dry land. The picture shows that many people at this time had little idea of what a whale looked like. The artist has drawn a creature with shark-like teeth and a long, curly tail.

LEAPING DOLPHINS

A pair of bottlenose dolphins leap effortlessly several metres out of the water. Their sleek, smooth-skinned bodies glisten in the sunlight. Powerful muscles near the tail provide them with the energy for fast swimming and leaping. Dolphins leap for various reasons – to signal to each other, to look for fish or perhaps just to have fun.

barnacles on humpback whale

whale lice

LOUSY WHALES

The skin of the grey whale is covered with light-coloured patches. These patches are clusters of lice, about 2 to 3cm long. These ten-legged creatures, called cyamids, feed on the whale's skin. All the large whales have lice, which are often found around clusters of barnacles on the skin.

HANGERS ON

As a humpback whale pokes its head out of the water here, you can see its throat. It is not as smooth as it might be because it is covered with barnacles. They are able to take hold on the whale's body because it is quite a slow-moving animal. They cannot easily grip the bodies of swifter-moving cetaceans, such as most dolphins. A dolphin sloughs rough skin away as it moves through the water. This also makes it harder for a barnacle to take hold.

melon-headed whales

Did you know? Whales have whiskers on their faces.

BODY LINES

A pod, or group, of melon-headed whales swim in the Pacific Ocean. This species is one of the smaller whales, at less than 3m long. It shows the features of a typical cetacean – the body is well rounded with a shortened neck and has only a single fin on its back. It has a pair of paddle-like front flippers and a tail with horizontal flukes. Cetaceans have no outer ears or back limbs.

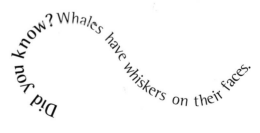

STAYING ALIVE

Like all mammals, whales are warm-blooded creatures. To stay alive, they must keep their bodies at a temperature of about 36–37°C. The trouble is that they swim in very cold water, often in temperatures of only a few degrees. The water quickly takes heat away from the surface of their bodies. To stop too much body heat getting to the surface, whales have a thick layer of a fatty substance called blubber just beneath the skin. This acts as insulation and holds in the heat.

Like other mammals, whales must breathe in order to stay alive. They breathe through nostrils known as blowholes. Unlike mammals' nostrils, a whale's blowhole is situated on top of the head, not in front. When a whale blows, or breathes out, it sends a column of steamy water vapour high into the air.

southern right whale

IN THE WARM

A southern right whale leaps out of the water in a magnificent display called breaching. This whale spends the summer feeding in ice-cold Antarctic waters. The sheer size of the whale helps limit the percentage of the body heat it loses to the water.

epidermis

layer of blubber

blood vessels

SKIN DEEP

This is a cross-section of the thick outer layer that covers a whale's body. Beneath a thin skin there is a thick layer of fatty blubber, which insulates the whale from ice-cold water.

SMALL SPECIES

Two Atlantic spotted dolphins play follow-my-leader. This species is among the smaller cetaceans. They are about the size of a human. Because it is quite small, its body has a relatively large surface area for its size and therefore loses heat faster than its big relatives. This is probably why the Atlantic spotted dolphin lives in quite warm waters.

Atlantic spotted dolphins

Did you know? The temperature of a whale is about the same as yours.

SKY HIGH

In the waters of Frederick Sound, in Alaska, a humpback whale surfaces and blows. The column of warm, moist air shoots high above the water. As it rises, it is cooled by the surrounding air. The moisture in it condenses into a cloud of tiny water droplets.

DEEP DIVING

Whales feed at different depths. Most dolphins feed on shoaling fish quite close to the surface. They never stay under water for more than 15 minutes. Blue whales can dive deeper, but not for much longer. The sperm whale holds the diving record, being able to descend to about 2,000m and stay under water for up to an hour.

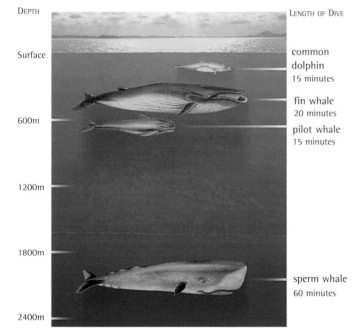

DEPTH		LENGTH OF DIVE
Surface		common dolphin 15 minutes
600m		fin whale 20 minutes
		pilot whale 15 minutes
1200m		
1800m		
		sperm whale 60 minutes
2400m		

humpback whale

ONE BLOWHOLE

A bottlenose dolphin rises to the surface to blow. It has only one blowhole, like all of the toothed whales. Here, the blowhole is seen open. When the dolphin dives, thick lips of elastic tissue will close it shut and prevent water entering, no matter how deep the dive or how high the water pressure.

bottlenose dolphin

TWO BLOWHOLES

These are the blowholes of a humpback whale. The humpback breathes out through a pair of blowholes, which are located behind a raised ridge called a splashguard. This helps prevent water entering the blowholes when the whale is blowing.

WHALE BRAIN AND SENSES

Like all animals, the whale controls its body through its nervous system. The brain is the control centre, carrying out many functions automatically, but also acting upon information supplied by the senses. The size of the whale brain varies greatly, according to the size of the animal. However, the dolphins have much bigger brains for their size, almost matching those of humans. Dolphins appear to be remarkably intelligent. Whales have the same five senses as we do, although their senses of taste and smell seem very limited. Hearing is by far their most important sense. They pick up sounds with tiny ears located just behind the eyes.

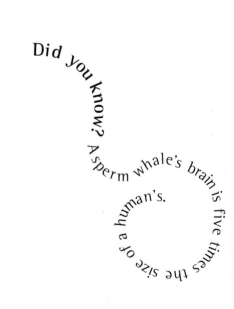

TINY EYES

Compared with its large body, a whale's eyes are tiny. It can see quite well when it is on the surface and often spy-hops, or lifts its head out of the water to look around. But when it dives deep for food, its eyes are useless in the dark water.

Atlantic spotted dolphins

Did you know? A sperm whale's brain is five times the size of a human's.

CLOSE ENCOUNTERS

A group of Atlantic spotted dolphins swim closely together in the seas around the Bahama Islands. Like most other cetaceans, the dolphins often nudge one another and stroke each other with their flippers and tail. Touch plays a very important part in dolphin society, especially in courtship.

SLAP HAPPY

A humpback whale slapping its tail, or lob-tailing, a favourite pastime for the great whales. It has raised up its tail and is about to slap it on to the water. This will create a noise like a gunshot in the air, but, more importantly, it will make a loud report underwater. All the other whales in the area will be able to hear the noise. Hearing is the most important sense in most whales.

CUPIDS AND DOLPHINS

In this beautiful Roman mosaic, cupids and dolphins gambol together in the sea. In Roman mythology, Cupid was the god of love, who shot arrows of passion from his bow. Roman artists were inspired by the dolphin's intelligence and gentleness with human beings. They regarded dolphins as sacred creatures.

humpback whale

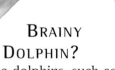

BRAINY DOLPHIN?

Some dolphins, such as the bottlenose, have a brain that is much the same size as our own. It is quite a complex brain with many folds – but still has a lot fewer folds than a human brain. Although the dolphin has a big brain, it is not necessarily highly intelligent.

bottlenose dolphin and trainer

IN TRAINING

A bottlenose dolphin is shown with its trainer at the Institute of Marine Sciences at Roatan, Honduras, in Central America. This species has a particularly large brain for its size. It can be easily trained, has a good memory and is a superb mimic. A bottlenose dolphin can observe other animals and learn to mimic their behaviour in a short space of time. It is also good at solving problems, something we consider a sign of intelligence.

SOUNDS AND SONGS

Sounds travel easily in water, and sounds are vital to whales. They use sounds to communicate with one another, and many use sounds to find their food. The large baleen whales use low-pitched sounds for communication. Underwater microphones have picked these sounds up as moans, grunts and snores. The humpback whale is the most vocal of the baleen whales, producing many kinds of sounds and stringing them together to make complicated songs. The toothed whales make higher-pitched sounds. These sounds are picked up as squeaks, creaks or whistles. Whales also use high-pitched clicks when hunting. They send out beams of sound, which are reflected by objects in their path, such as fish. The whale picks up the reflected sound, or echo, and can work out the object's location. This is called echo-location.

Amazon river dolphin

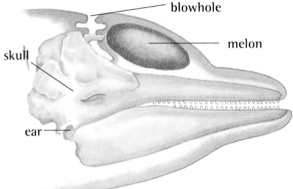

ECHO SOUNDINGS

The Amazon river dolphin, or boto, hunts by means of echo-location. It sends out high pitched clicking sounds, making up to 80 clicks every second. The sound is transmitted in a broad beam from a bulge, called a melon, on top of its head. All toothed whales and dolphins hunt in this way. Most have narrower, but more advanced, sound systems.

MAKING WAVES

A dolphin makes high-pitched sound waves by vibrating the air in the passages in its nose. The waves are focused into a beam by the melon – the bulge on top of its head. The beam of sound is transmitted into the water.

group of belugas

SEA CANARIES

A group of belugas, or white whales, swim in the shallows of a bay in northern Canada. Belugas are noisy creatures whose voices can clearly be heard above the surface. This is why they are sometimes called sea canaries. Belugas also produce high-pitched sounds we cannot hear, which they use for echo-location.

humpback whale

SUPER SONGSTER
It is the breeding season, and this male humpback whale is heading for the breeding grounds where the females are gathering. The male starts singing long and complicated songs. This may be to announce its arrival and to attract a mate, or it could be to warn other males off its patch. The sound of these songs can carry for 30km or more.

LONG SONGS
This is a voice print of a humpback whale singing a song. The sounds have been picked up underwater by a hydrophone, or underwater microphone. Prints like these show complex musical phrases and melodies. Humpback whales often continue singing for a day or more, with the animals repeating the same basic song time and time again.

SOUND ECHOES
One of the most exciting underwater battles is that of a sperm whale wrestling with a giant squid. The whale can locate a squid more than a kilometre away by transmitting pulses of sound waves into the water and listening. The returning echo is picked up by the teeth in the lower jaw. The vibrations are sent along the jaw to the ear.

Did you know? A dolphin picks up sounds through its lower jaw.

Did you know? A blue whale's long moans are the loudest sound of any animal.

Voyager space probe

sperm whale

giant squid

ALIEN GREETINGS
The songs of the humpback whale not only travel through Earth's oceans, but they are also travelling far out into Space. They are among the recorded typical sounds of our world that are being carried by the two Voyager space probes. These probes are now many millions of kilometres away from Earth and are on their way to the stars.

FEEDING HABITS

CRUNCHY KRILL

These creatures are known as krill. Like crabs and shrimps, they are crustaceans. They form the main part of the diet of many baleen whales, especially in Antarctica. Measuring up to 75mm long, they swim in vast shoals, often covering an area of several square kilometres. Most krill are found in Antarctic waters.

The two main groups of whales eat quite different food. Most of the huge baleen whales feed by taking great mouthfuls of seawater containing fish and tiny shrimp-like creatures called krill or plankton, as well as algae, jellyfish, worms and so on. The whale closes its mouth and lifts its tongue, forcing water out through the bristly baleen plates on the upper jaw. The baleen acts like a sieve and holds back the plankton or fish, which the whale then swallows. The toothed whales feed mainly on fish and squid. They find their prey by echo-location. It is essential for species like the sperm whale, which dive deep into the ocean where it is dark. Some toothed whales hunt in packs.

grey whale

PLOUGHED FOOD

A grey whale ploughs into the seabed, stirring up the sand and ooze. It also dislodges the tiny crustaceans that live there and gulps them down. These crustaceans, called amphipods, are only about 15mm long. Grey whales feed mostly during summer in the Arctic region before they migrate further south.

southern right whale

SKIM FEEDING

With its mouth open, a southern right whale cruises slowly over the surface of the sea. It filters tiny crustaceans, called copepods, out of the water with its fine baleen. It can eat as much as two tonnes of these plankton every day. It needs to eat so much because of its huge size - up to 80 tonnes. Usually right whales feed alone, but if food is plentiful, several will feed cruising side by side.

SUCCULENT SQUID

A shoal of squid swim in Californian waters. Squid is the sperm whale's favourite food and is eaten by other toothed whales and dolphins as well. Squid are molluscs, in the same animal phylum as snails and octopuses. But, unlike octopuses, they have eight arms and two tentacles, and are therefore called decapods (meaning ten feet). Squid swim together in dense shoals, many thousand strong. They are fast swimmers. There are many species of squid, measuring from a few centimetres long up to 20m in the case of the giant squid.

TOOTHY SMILE

A Ganges river dolphin shows its teeth. The front teeth are visible even when its mouth is closed because they are particularly long. In all, the dolphin has more than 100 teeth. Ganges river dolphins eat mainly fish, but they also take shrimp and crab. They usually feed at night and find their prey by echo-location.

Did you know? A blue whale eats nearly 1,000kg of krill in a single meal.

Ganges river dolphin

sperm whale

BELUGA LUNCH

Belugas, or white whales, feed on squid and small fish, which are in plentiful supply in their icy ocean home. Unlike common dolphins, belugas do not have many teeth. Scientists think that many squid-eating whales may simply suck prey into their mouths. Many species of beaked whale, which also feed on squid, have no teeth suitable for clutching prey.

beluga whale

HUNT THE SQUID

This sperm whale is hunting. It is the largest toothed whale, notable for its huge head and tiny lower jaw. The sperm whale feeds in deep water on squid. It often hunts the giant squid that live in waters around 2,000m deep. At that depth, in total darkness, the sperm whale hunts its prey by sonar, or echo-location.

IN FOR THE KILL

Among the toothed whales, the killer whale, or orca, is the master predator. It feeds on a wider variety of prey than any other whale. It bites and tears its prey to pieces with its fearsome teeth and may also batter them with its powerful tail. It is the only whale to take warm-blooded prey. Fortunately, there is no record of a killer whale ever attacking human beings. However, wildlife watchers and photographers often report killer whales spy-hopping when they approach, as though sizing them up for a meal. As well as fish and squid, a killer whale will hunt seals, penguins, dolphins and porpoises. It may even attack large baleen whales many times its size. Killer whales live in family groups, or pods, which often go hunting together. Cooperative hunting greatly improves the chance of success. But killer whales will also go hunting by themselves when they chance upon a likely victim, such as a lone sea lion.

THE ATTACK BEGINS

A hungry killer whale has spotted a sea lion splashing in the surf at the water's edge. With powerful strokes of its tail, it surges towards its intended prey. The whale's tall dorsal fin shows that it is a fully-grown male. The sea lion seems totally unaware of what is happening but, in any case, it is nearly helpless in the shallow water. The killer is scraping the shore as it homes in for the kill.

TERRIBLE TEETH

Suddenly the killer's head bursts out of the water, and its jaws gape open. Its vicious teeth are exposed, ready to sink into its sea lion prey. The killer whale may have fewer teeth than most toothed whales, but they are large and very strong.

NO ESCAPE

Now the killer snaps its jaws shut, clamping the sea lion in a vice-like grip. With its prey struggling helplessly, it slides back into deep water to eat its fill. Killer whales sometimes almost beach themselves when they lunge after prey but, helped by the surf, they usually manage to wriggle their way back into the sea.

LUNGING FOR LUNCH

The humpback whale is a filter-feeder, taking in great mouthfuls of water and filtering out the food in them through its baleen plates. Usually it scoops up the water as it lunges forwards and upwards. This way of lunge-feeding is typical of the baleen whales known as the rorquals, which also include the blue, fin, sei and minke whales. All these whales have grooves in their throats, which allow the mouth to expand greatly. This, in turn, enables them to take in many tonnes of water containing their food. Sometimes, before lunge-feeding, humpbacks may round up the fish by blowing a circle of bubbles around them. The bubbles act like a net and stop the fish escaping.

ON THE LOOKOUT

Poking its head out of the water, a humpback whale spy-hops in the feeding grounds of Alaska. It is looking for signs of shoals of fish, such as anchovy and cod. Here, in the Northern Hemisphere, humpbacks feed mainly on fish. The Southern Hemisphere population of humpbacks feed mainly on plankton, such as krill.

FORWARD LUNGE

Once it has located a shoal, the humpback swims towards it. In the middle of the shoal, it opens its enormous mouth and lunges forwards. The throat grooves in the bottom jaw expand as the water – and the fish – rush in. Next, the humpback uses its tongue and cheek muscles to force out the water through its baleen plates, leaving the fish behind in its mouth.

UPWARD LUNGE

Here, the humpback is using a different technique. It sinks below the surface and then flicks its tail to help it to shoot upwards again. With mouth gaping open, it lunges at the fish from below.

RING OF BUBBLES

The surface of the sea is boiling with a ring of frothy bubbles. Unseen, beneath the water, one or more humpback whales are swimming round in circles, letting out air as they do so.

BUBBLE NETTING

The circle of bubbles rises up to the surface from the whales circling under the water. It forms a kind of net around a shoal of fish and prevents the fish inside from escaping. The whales then swim upwards to the surface with their mouths gaping, ready to engulf the netted prey.

humpback whale

SWIMMING

All the whales are superb swimmers. Even the huge baleen whales can swim faster than an Olympic swimmer. All parts of the whale's body help it move through the water. The driving force comes from the tail fin, or flukes. Using very powerful muscles in the rear third of its body, the whale beats its tail up and down. The whole body bends when this happens. The whale uses its pectoral fins, or flippers, near the front of the body to steer with. The body itself has a streamlined shape and is very smooth to help it slip through the water easily with the least drag, or resistance. The body has some flexibility and can change shape slightly to keep the water flowing smoothly around it. Little ridges under the skin help as well. Some whales also give out tiny droplets of oil from their skin, which further reduces drag.

STEERING

Among whales, the humpback has by far the longest front flippers. Whales use their paddle-like flippers mainly for steering as they travel through the water. The humpback also uses its flippers for slapping the water. Flipper-slapping seems to be some form of communication.

grey whale's
tail flukes

TAIL POWER
The tail flukes of a grey whale rise into the air before it dives. Whales move their broad tails up and down to drive themselves through the water.

killer whale
with dorsal fin raised

MASSIVE FIN
The dorsal fin of a killer whale projects high into the air. The animal is a swift swimmer, and the fin helps keep its body well balanced as it travels through the water. The killer whale has such a large dorsal fin that some experts believe it may help to regulate their body temperature, or even be used in courtship. Most whales and dolphins have a dorsal fin, although some only have a raised hump on their back.

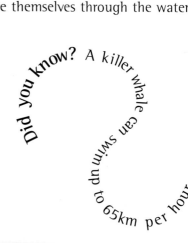

Did you know? A killer whale can swim up to 65km per hour.

Atlantic spotted dolphins

STREAMLINING

Atlantic spotted dolphins swim without effort in their underwater habitat. Their bodies are beautifully streamlined. This means they are shaped so that they slip easily through the water when they move. The dolphin's body is long and rounded, relatively broad in front and becoming narrower towards the tail. Apart from the dorsal fin on the dolphin's back, and flippers, nothing projects from its body. It has no external ears or rear limbs, and the sexual organs are usually hidden under folds of skin.

bottlenose dolphin

HOW A DOLPHIN SWIMS

Like all the cetaceans, dolphins use their tails to propel themselves through the water. They beat their tail flukes up and down by means of the powerful muscles near the tail. The flukes force the water backwards at each stroke, and as the water is forced back, the body of the dolphin is forced forwards. The other fins on the dolphin's body help guide it through the water. They do not supply any swimming power.

SMOOTH SKINNED

This bottlenose dolphin is tailwalking – supporting itself by powerful thrusts of its tail. As can be seen, it has an amazingly smooth skin. Unlike most other mammals, it has no covering of hair or hair follicles – the little dimples in the skin from which the hair grows. Its very smooth skin helps the dolphin's body slip easily through the water.

dolphin swimming

HOW A FISH SWIMS

A fish has similar fins to a dolphin and, like a dolphin, it is mainly the tail that provides the power for swimming. A fish's tail has vertical fins, unlike the horizontal fins of the dolphin. The fish swims by beating its tail and body from side to side, not up and down like a dolphin.

fish swimming

Swimming

25

READY, STEADY, DIVE!

Most whales feed beneath the surface, some often diving deep to reach their food. We can usually identify the species of whale from the way it prepares to dive, or sound. The sperm whale, for example, is one of the species that lifts its tail high into the air before it descends into the ocean depths. It is the deepest diver of all the whales, sometimes descending to more than a kilometre in search of squid. It can remain under water for 60 minutes or more before it has to come up for air. As in other whales, its lungs collapse when it dives. It is thought that the great mass of oil in its huge head helps the whale when diving and surfacing. The oil freezes and becomes heavier on the way down, then melts and becomes lighter again on the way up.

BLOWING

Two sperm whales swimming at the surface. The one on the left is preparing to dive. Its head is in the air, and it is filling its lungs with air in a series of blows. The sperm whale's blow is easy to recognize because the spout projects forwards, as in no other whale.

SPURTING

Seen from above, the diving whale lashes its tail and accelerates through the water, creating a foaming wake. Its head goes under. If it is going to make a deep dive, the whale may not take another breath for over an hour.

ARCHING

Now the whale starts the dive, thrusting its bulbous head down and arching its back steeply. The rounded hump on its back rises high into the air. The lumpy knuckles behind the hump become visible as the body arches over.

FLUKING

Soon the body disappears with just the tail flukes poking out of the water. The body is now in a vertical position and that is how it remains as the whale dives swiftly into the deep. Descending at speeds of more than 150m per minute, it is soon in darkness, scanning its surroundings by beams of sound for the squid on which it feeds.

SOCIAL LIFE

In our daily lives, we meet, work, play and communicate with many other people. We are part of human society. We are sociable animals. Some kinds of whales are also very sociable and live together in groups. Sperm whales, for example, live in groups of up to about 50. A group may be a breeding school of females and young or a bachelor school of young males. The older male sperm whales spend much of their time alone, except during the breeding season. Beluga whales have a similar kind of organization. Belugas often live in groups of several hundred, as do some kinds of dolphins. The baleen whales are not as sociable. They tend to move about singly or in small family groups. This is probably because of their enormous appetite – they could not find enough food if they lived close together all the time.

HERD INSTINCT
beluga whales

Beluga whales gather together in very large groups, or herds, and they mostly stay in these herds for life. Many of the animals in this group, pictured in the Canadian Arctic, have calves. These can be recognized, not only by their smaller size, but also by their darker skin colour.

Did you know? Dolphins will nudge a sick member of the group up to the surface, so it does not drown.

NOSEY ORCAS
Two killer whales, or orcas, spy-hop in Antarctic waters. They rise out of the water together, as if on a signal. They are members of the same pod, which stay together all their lives. The bonds between the animals are very strong. This helps them coordinate their activities, especially when hunting for food.

killer whales

Atlantic spotted dolphins

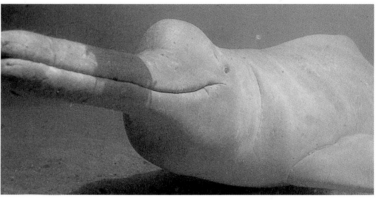

STAYING CLOSE
Two Atlantic spotted dolphins swim with their young. The young have no spots and are smaller. Spots do not start to appear until the animals are about a year old. As with many other species, the young stay very close to their parents most of the time. Spotted dolphins are usually found in quite small groups of less than 20.

HUMAN CONTACT
A bottlenose dolphin swims alongside a boy. These dolphins live in social groups but lone outcasts, or animals that have become separated from their group, often approach humans.

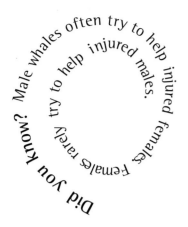

Amazon river dolphin

SOLITARY SWIMMER
An Amazon river dolphin, or boto, is resting on the river bed. It may spend most of its life by itself, or maybe with just one other animal. This solitary behaviour is typical of the other river dolphins too. They are not sociable animals like most other whales and dolphins.

PILOT ERROR
Long-finned pilot whales are stranded on a beach in Tasmania. Pilot whales usually live in large groups, and there are strong bonds between group members. This can lead to the disaster of mass stranding. One of the whales may get into difficulties and strand itself on the beach. The other members of the pod try to help it and become stranded themselves.

long-finned pilot whales

THE MATING GAME

Like most other mammals, whales court one another and mate at a certain time of the year. Baleen whales, for example, mate during the late autumn after the whales have migrated to their warm-water breeding grounds. One whale will mate a number of times with different partners. Sometimes several males will attempt to manoeuvre a female into a mating position. Often the males fight each other for the chance to mate, biting, headbutting or lashing their tails at one another. Male narwhals fence one another with their long tusks. But mating behaviour can also be gentle, with the males and females caressing one another with their flippers.

grey whale

beluga whales

WHITE WEDDING

A pair of belugas begin to take an interest in each other. Male and female belugas spend much of the year in separate groups, only mixing during the mating season in the summer in northern waters. Mating and calving (about 14 months later) take place in shallow bays in the far north.

LOVE SONGS

Like other mammals, whales attract a mate by body language and sound. Amazingly, whales such as this humpback can pinpoint each other's position, and perhaps exchange messages, through the ocean over great distances.

humpback whale

MATING BRAWL

Two grey whales court in the winter breeding grounds in the seas off Baja California, Mexico. Usually, a group of males fights furiously for the right to mate with a female, causing a lot of commotion in the water. The female might mate many times with her battling escorts.

ROLLOVER

Courtship for these southern right whales is nearly over. The male *(top)* has succeeded in getting the female to roll over on her back and is manoeuvring into the mating position. This scene is in the Valdez Peninsula, Argentina, the winter breeding grounds for southern right whales.

southern right whales

THE FABULOUS UNICORN

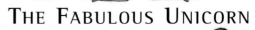

In the breeding season, male narwhals fight one another using their long tusks, which often break. In ancient times, when these small whales were little known, people found these tusks and wondered what kind of beast they came from. This may have led to the idea of the unicorn, usually shown as a horse-like creature with a long spiral horn (like the narwhal's) on its forehead.

BELLY TO BELLY

A pair of southern right whales mate, belly to belly. The male has inserted his long penis into the female to inject his sperm. Usually, the male's penis stays hidden in the body behind a genital slit. It will be nine months or more before the female gives birth to a single calf.

BIG BABY

A sperm whale calf snuggles up to its mother, almost as if the two are stuck together. A calf might measure up to 4.5m long when born, nearly 15 months after mating took place. The mother feeds it for a year or more, leaving it alone only when diving deep for food.

sperm whale and calf

Did you know? Female sperm whales can mate at the age of 8. Males cannot mate until they are nearly 20.

BRINGING UP BABY

BIRTHDAY
A bottlenose dolphin gives birth to her baby. The baby is being born tail-first, the usual way. It has been growing inside the mother's body for about a year, and is now nearly 1m long. This birth is taking place near the bottom of an aquarium. In the wild, birth takes place close to the surface so the baby can surface quickly and start to breathe.

After a successful mating, the female whale becomes pregnant and a baby whale starts to grow inside her body. After about a year, the baby (calf) is ready to be born. By now it can weigh, in the case of the blue whale, up to 2.5 tonnes. The first thing the calf must do is take a breath, and the mother or another whale may help it up to the surface. Soon it finds one of the mother's nipples and starts to suck the thick, rich milk in her mammary glands (breasts). It will continue to suckle for several months until it learns to take solid food such as fish. Mother and calf may spend most of the time by themselves, or join nursery schools with other mothers and calves. The beluga and sperm whales are known for their nursery schools. When a sperm whale mother has to dive for food, an aunt looks after her calf.

SUCKLING
A beluga mother suckles her young under water. The mother's milk has a high fat content and is very nutritious, and the calf grows rapidly. It will continue to drink milk for up to two years. At birth the calf's body is dark grey in colour, but it gradually lightens as the calf matures.

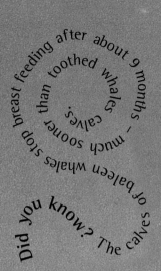

AT PLAY

A young Atlantic spotted dolphin and its mother play together, twisting, turning, rolling and touching each other with their flippers. During play, the young dolphin learns the skills it will need later in life when it has to fend for itself. The youngster is darker than its mother and has no spots. These do not start to appear until it is about a year old.

Did you know? The calves of baleen whales stop breast feeding after about 9 months – much sooner than toothed whales' calves.

TOGETHERNESS

A humpback whale calf sticks closely to its mother as she swims slowly in Hawaiian waters. The slipstream, or water flow, created by the mother's motion helps pull it along. For the first few months of its life, it will not stray far from its mother's side.

HAVING FUN

Dolphins have delighted people with their acrobatic antics for thousands of years. They were a favourite subject for ancient Greek and Roman artists, for example. They leap, spin and somersault, ride the bow waves of boats and go surfing. The spinner and dusky dolphins are particularly lively, hurling themselves high into the air. Some dolphin antics undoubtedly have a purpose, such as sending signals to other dolphins. But often the animals appear to perform acrobatics just for fun during their playtime. In most animal species it is the young that play. In whale and dolphin society, the adults play too. One of the games southern right whales play is sailing. They hang vertically in the water with their heads down and tails in the air. The tails act like sails and catch the wind, and they are blown along.

Atlantic spotted dolphins

PLAYFUL PAIR
Two Atlantic spotted dolphins jostle one another as they play with a type of coral, called a sea fan. Dolphins spend much of their time playing, especially the younger ones. They seem to make up all kinds of games, using anything they can find, such as pieces of driftwood, leaves, feathers and stones. Sometimes their games last for hours.

JUMPING FOR JOY
A pair of bottlenose dolphins leaps high into the air. They leave the water at exactly the same time, as though they have been rehearsing their act for the photographer. They seem to be jumping just for the joy of it, but their behaviour may have some kind of social function within their family group.

bottlenose dolphins

PORPOISING ON PURPOSE

A group of long-snouted spinner dolphins go porpoising, taking long, low leaps as they swim swiftly. As you can see, they churn the water behind them into a foam. Many dolphins practise porpoising, which is a more efficient method of travelling fast on the surface.

Did you know? Killer whales like brushing against each other as they swim at high speed.

long-snouted spinner dolphins

Pacific white-sided dolphin

RIDING THE WAKE

This picture shows a Pacific white-sided dolphin surfing on the waves. This is one of the most active and acrobatic of the dolphins. It is also often seen bow-riding in front of boats. Many other species of dolphins also like to ride in the foam and waves left in the wake of passing boats.

Did you know? The rough skin on a porpoise's back may be for giving calves piggy-back rides.

dusky dolphin

Did you know? A dolphin may play cat and mouse with its prey before eating it.

AQUATIC ACROBAT

This dusky dolphin is in a playful mood, throwing itself high into the air. It twists and turns, spins and performs somersaults. It is one of the most acrobatic of all the dolphins. This behaviour is like a roll call – to check that every dolphin in the group is present and ready to go hunting. This behaviour is repeated after hunting to gather the group together once more.

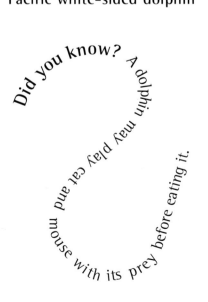

WHALES ON DISPLAY

One of the most spectacular sights in nature is of the great whales leaping out of the water and crashing back to the surface amid a shower of spray. This activity is called breaching. It is common among humpbacks. Some animals have been observed to breach up to 200 times in succession. When one whale starts breaching, others start breaching too. Like other whales, humpbacks put on other displays as well, including slapping their flippers and tail on the surface. These activities make a lot of noise, particularly underwater. They could, like breaching, be some form of signalling. Spy-hopping is another common activity among most whales. It is often done to look for signs of fish to eat.

BREACHING

Propelled by powerful thrusts of its tail, the humpback launches its vast bulk into the air, twisting as it does so. For a creature weighing up to 30 tonnes, this is no mean feat. As breaching ends, the humpback crashes back to the surface with a splash. This time it lands on its back, with one of its flippers up in the air.

FLIPPER-FLOPPING

The humpback swims on the surface, raising one of its long flippers in the air. Then it rolls over and slaps the flipper on the water. It may do this several times in succession, perhaps to warn off rivals. The humpback's flipper-flopping (or flipper-slapping) is particularly noisy because its flippers are so large.

WHAT A FLUKE!

The humpback raises its tail in the air during the display known as lob-tailing or tail-slapping. The tail is also exposed when the whale is about to dive, behaviour called fluking. It is easy to tell if a humpback is lob-tailing or fluking. In fluking, the tail disappears below the surface quietly.

LOB-TAILING

In lob-tailing the tail is brought down sharply on to the surface of the water in a shower of spray and with a noise like a gunshot. Apart from when it is lob-tailing, the humpback only shows its flukes when it is about to go on a deep dive.

SPY-HOPPING

The humpback on the right of the picture is spy-hopping. It positions itself vertically in the water and pokes out its head until its eyes are showing. Then it has a good look round. The other humpback here is doing the opposite, poking out its tail, ready to lob-tail.

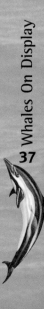

WHERE WHALES ARE FOUND

Whales of one kind or another are found in all the oceans of the world. Some species of whale range widely, while others are found only in a certain area. They may stay in the same place all year long, or they may migrate from one area to another with the seasons. There are whales that stick to shallow coastal waters, and those that prefer the deep waters of the open ocean. Some live in the cool waters of far northern or far southern parts of the world, or at high latitudes. Others are more at home in tropical regions near the Equator or in low latitudes. You will find some kind of whale or dolphin in practically all parts of the oceans. There are even some species living in rivers.

OCEAN WANDERER

A humpback whale surfaces to blow while swimming at Cape Cod off the north-east coast of North America. The humpback is found in all the oceans, but in different places at different times. In summer it remains in high latitudes feeding. Then it migrates thousands of kilometres to low latitudes to breed during the winter months.

MUDDY WATERS

The mud-laden waters of the River Amazon in South America are the habitat of the largest river dolphin, the Amazon river dolphin. Here, one is showing its fine set of teeth. This species ranges along the Amazon and its tributaries, and throughout the Orinoco River system to the north.

killer whale

Did you know? Some dolphins come and go between salt water and fresh water.

WORLDWIDE KILLER

Among ice-floes in the Arctic Ocean, a killer whale hunts for prey. Killer whales may be found in all oceans of the world, from the high Arctic to the Antarctic. They live in coastal areas but sometimes venture out to the open ocean. Killer whales also swim inshore among the surf, sometimes even beaching to snatch their prey.

SNOW WHITE

These belugas, or white whales, are swimming in Hudson Bay, Canada. They are cold-water creatures, living around the coasts in the far north of North America, Europe and Asia. They venture into estuaries and even up rivers, such as the Mackenzie River in Canada. In winter they hunt among the pack ice in the Arctic.

beluga whales

melon-headed whales

TROPICAL MELONS

A pod of melon-headed whales is shown swimming in the Pacific Ocean. These creatures prefer warm waters and are found in subtropical and tropical regions in both the Northern and Southern Hemispheres. They generally stay in deep water, keeping well away from land.

Did you know? Several species of beaked whale have been so elusive that no one has seen them alive.

bottlenose dolphin

WIDE RANGER

A bottlenose dolphin lunges through the surf in the sunny Bahamas. This animal is one of the most wide-ranging of the dolphins, being found in temperate to tropical waters in both the Northern and Southern Hemispheres. It is also found in enclosed seas such as the Mediterranean and Red Sea. Mostly it stays in coastal waters. When bottlenose dolphins migrate to warmer areas, they lose weight. When they return to colder climes, they gain more blubber.

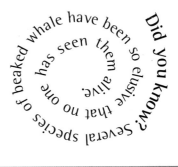

MIGRATION

Grey whales spend the summer months feeding in the food-rich waters of the Arctic Ocean. Many of the females are pregnant. Before winter comes, the whales head south towards Mexico for warmer waters, where the females will give birth to their calves. In the warmer climate, the calves stand a better chance of surviving. Mating also takes place around late winter. When spring comes, the greys begin to head north to the Arctic. Their annual journey between their feeding and breeding grounds is one of the greatest animal migrations, involving a round trip of some 20,000km. The northern and southern populations of humpbacks take part in long migrations too. Most of the other large rorquals and the right whales seem to undergo similar migrations from cold water feeding grounds to warm water breeding grounds. Among dolphins, which live mostly in warmer waters, there is little evidence of such large-scale migrations.

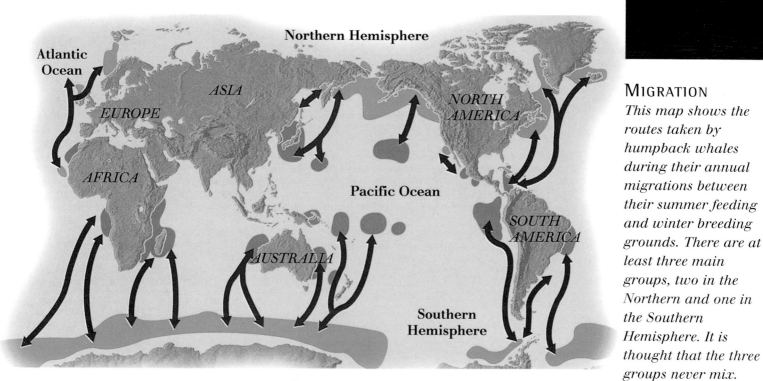

MIGRATION

This map shows the routes taken by humpback whales during their annual migrations between their summer feeding and winter breeding grounds. There are at least three main groups, two in the Northern and one in the Southern Hemisphere. It is thought that the three groups never mix.

KEY TO MAP

   breeding grounds   *feeding grounds*

SUMMER FEEDING

Two Southern Hemisphere humpbacks feed in the rich waters of the Antarctic Ocean during the summer months. This is when the krill and other plankton they feed on thrive. These two whales have just taken large mouthfuls of water, which they will now sieve for plankton using the baleen on their upper jaws.

Southern Hemisphere humpbacks

humpback whales

RIGHT LOCATION

The tail fluke of a southern right whale is thrust into the air as the whale sails. This whale is one of a group of right whales in winter breeding grounds off the coast of Argentina in South America. By summer the whales will have returned south to feed in the Antarctic Ocean.

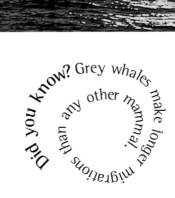

southern right whale

Did you know? Grey whales make longer migrations than any other mammal.

WINTER BREEDING

It is early winter in the Southern Hemisphere, and these two humpbacks have spent the past weeks migrating north from the Antarctic. They have arrived at their destination in a shallow bay on the coast of eastern Australia. It is here that one large group of humpbacks have their breeding grounds. Here they will mate and, about 12 months later, the females will give birth.

MATING GREYS

In the winter breeding grounds of Baja California, a grey whale surfaces near a boatload of whale-watchers. Grey whales spend about three months in the region, where mating and (two years later) births take place. They take some three months to migrate north back to Arctic waters.

grey whale

HIGH AND DRY

Dead whales, large and small, are often found washed up, or stranded, on the seashore. Live whales are sometimes found too, particularly open ocean species, such as pilot whales and sperm whales. Some live whales probably strand when they become ill and weak. Others may strand when they lose their sense of direction.

It is thought that whales may navigate, or find their way around, using the Earth's magnetism as a kind of map. Slight changes in this magnetism might cause them to turn the wrong way and head for the shore. Sometimes mass strandings take place, with scores of whales left helpless. This happens particularly among sociable species, such as the pilot whales. It is believed that when one animal gets stranded and becomes distressed, the other whales travelling with it try to help and become stranded too.

Did you know? When people help stranded whales, the whales often swim back and get stranded again.

Atlantic white-sided dolphin

BEACHED DOLPHIN
This Atlantic white-sided dolphin is stranded on a beach in the Orkney Islands. Strandings are quite common in this species. The dolphins usually travel in quite large groups, so mass strandings can sometimes take place too.

WAITING FOR THE TIDE
People come to the assistance of more than 60 stranded long-finned pilot whales on the beach at Golden Bay, New Zealand. People cover the whales to stop them becoming sunburnt and throw water over them to keep their skin moist.

RARE STRANDING

Marine biologists examine a stranded Stejneger's beaked whale. Beaked whales are among the least known of all the cetaceans. Most of our knowledge about them comes from occasional strandings like this. Note the large tooth protruding from the jaws. Several beaked whales have teeth like this.

Stejneger's beaked whale

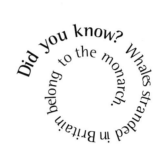

Did you know? Whales stranded in Britain belong to the monarch.

IN THE SHALLOWS

Three belugas, or white whales, are stranded in the shallow waters of a bay as the tide has gone out. They are vulnerable to attack from polar bears when beached like this. Belugas spend a lot of time swimming in shallow water, but do not usually become stranded. If they do, they can usually survive until the tide comes in again.

beluga whales

BIG FIN

A fin whale has become beached on a mudflat. As you can see, compared with a human, it is an enormous creature. Some fin whales can grow to 25m or more and weigh up to 80 tonnes. This animal is dead, but even if it were alive, it would be impossible to do anything to help it to return to the water. Its internal organs will collapse when the animal is not supported by the water. However, scientists can examine stranded bodies to learn new information about whales.

GREY AND RIGHT WHALES

Grey whales and the three species of right whale, including the bowhead, are all filter-feeders with baleen plates in their upper jaws. The bowhead has the longest baleen of all, while the grey has short baleen. Unlike most other baleen whales, however, the grey whale feeds mainly on the seabed. It is also noted for its long annual migration along the Pacific coast of North America from the Arctic to Mexican waters. The grey whale is found only in the Northern Hemisphere, but there are populations of right whales in both hemispheres. Right whales were named by whalers because they were the right whales to catch. They swam slowly, they could be approached easily and they floated when dead. Right whales yielded large amounts of oil and baleen.

Did you know? The bowhead whale has longer baleen than any other whale – over 4m long.

MOTTLED MAMMAL

The distinctive long, narrow head of a grey whale breaks the surface. Its closed blowholes are in the middle of the picture. The head is covered here and there with clusters of barnacles and lice, which are also found over many other parts of the body. This, together with lighter body patches, gives the whole animal a mottled appearance.

bowhead whale

WHITE CHIN

A bowhead whale thrusts its head out of the water, exposing its white chin patch. It is the only whale to have a white chin. This is covered with numerous black patches. The skin is smooth, with no growths like those on the skin of the northern and southern right whales.

Did you know? We know a lot about grey whales because they stay in shallow waters near the coast.

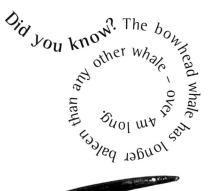

LIVELY LOB-TAILING

Near the coast of Argentina in South America, a southern right whale is lob-tailing. In seconds, its tail will come crashing down on the surface with a resounding smack that will echo off the cliffs on the shore. The noise will be heard by other whales, many kilometres away. Right whales often lob-tail and also do headstands, waving their tails in the air.

southern right whale

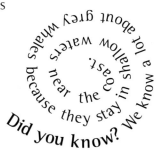

BEARD AND BONNET

A southern right whale cruises in the South Atlantic. Two features make this whale impossible to mistake. One is the deeply curved jawline. The other is the southern right whale's beard and bonnet. These are large growths on the whale's chin and nose, which become infested with barnacles.

southern right whale

northern right whale

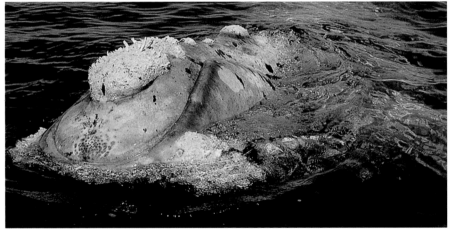

HAIRY MONSTER

There are two populations of right whale – the northern and southern right whale. The northern right whale, pictured here, lives in the North Atlantic. Whalers used to refer to the crusty hard skin on its head as its bonnet or rock garden. Barnacles and whale lice develop on this skin and it can grow to an enormous size. The right whale is also the hairiest of all whales, retaining more of its hair after birth than any other cetacean. It even grows facial hair in places where humans do!

grey whale

Did you know? You can tell a grey whale by its unique long, narrow head.

BRISTLY JAWS

A grey whale opens its mouth, showing the baleen plates on its upper jaw. The baleen is quite short, stiff and coarse. The whale uses it to filter out the tiny creatures it digs out of the seabed when feeding. Grey whales are not shy and sometimes swim up to the boats of whale-watchers.

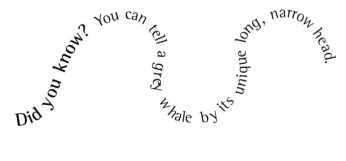

RORQUALS

The rorquals are a family of baleen whales that includes the largest creature that has ever lived on Earth, the blue whale. They are named after the grooves that they have on the throat – the word rorqual means a furrow. All rorquals, except the humpback, have a long streamlined body with a sharp nose and a dorsal fin set well back. They can all swim fast, reaching speeds up to about 30kph. The humpback is a slower swimmer with a chunkier body. It has long, knobbly flippers and a pronounced hump in front of the dorsal fin. The humpback is famous for the songs it sings. The minke whale is the smallest rorqual and is also the most common. Bryde's whale lives mainly in warm tropical and subtropical waters. The other rorquals are found in cold waters as well, often venturing into polar waters in the summer.

minke whale

TINY MINKE
The minke whale is the smallest rorqual. It grows to only about one-third of the size of the blue whale and never exceeds 10 tonnes in weight. It has a slim, smooth snout and a prominent curved dorsal fin. The minke's flippers are relatively short and are sometimes marked, as here, with a broad white band.

Did you know? Humpback whales can live to age 95.

WHALE WITH A HUMP
This picture of a humpback whale shows the feature that gives it its name very well. Its small dorsal fin sits on top of a pronounced hump on its back. This profile view of the animal also shows the prominent splash guard on its head in front of the blowholes. Note also the many knobs on the head and throat.

humpback whale

flipper

KNOBBLY FLIPPER
A humpback whale swims on the surface, with one of its flippers up in the air like a boat sail. The flippers of the humpback are by far the most distinctive of all the whales. They are sturdy and very long – up to a third of the length of the whale's body. The flippers have knobs along their leading (front) edge.

BIG GULP

A blue whale feeds in Californian waters. It has taken in a mouthful of water containing thousands of the tiny shrimp-like creatures it feeds on. The grooves on its throat that allow its mouth to expand can be clearly seen. A blue whale typically has between about 60 and 90 of these grooves.

blue whale

Did you know? A humpback whale may sing for 30 minutes at a time.

DRIPPING FLUKES

A blue whale fluking, with its tail flukes rising out of the water before the animal dives. Among the rorquals, only blue and humpback whales expose their flukes in this way before diving. The humpback's tail flukes are quite different. They are knobbly at the trailing (rear) edges and have white markings on the underside.

blue whale

Did you know? A blue whale's heart is about the size of a small car.

SEI WHALE

The sei whale can be found in most oceans. It feeds in the cool Arctic or Antarctic waters during the summer and migrates to warmer waters in the winter to breed. With a length of up to about 18m, it is slightly larger than the similar looking Bryde's whale.

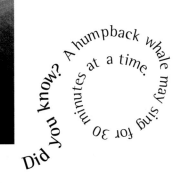

SPERM AND WHITE WHALES

The sperm and the white whales are two families of toothed whales. The sperm whale and dwarf and pygmy sperm whales have an organ in their head called the spermaceti organ, which is filled with wax. The wax may help the animals when they dive and may play a part in focusing the sound waves they use for echo-location. All three species spend most of their time in deep water. The sperm whale is similar in size to the large baleen whales. It has teeth on only its tiny lower jaw and no dorsal fin, just a hump. The two white whales, the beluga and the narwhal, also have no dorsal fin. The beluga has up to about 20 teeth in each of its jaws, but the narwhal has only two. In the male narwhal, one of the teeth grows into a long spiral tusk, measuring up to 3m.

BABY EYES

The eye of a sperm whale calf. Like all whales, the sperm whale has tiny eyes compared with those of most other mammals. But this does not matter because when the whale dives to feed, it descends deep into the ocean where light never reaches. It depends on its superb echo-location system to find its prey.

sperm whale

Did you know? Perfume is made from foul-smelling wax made in sperm whales' guts.

Did you know? A sperm whale can dive as deep as 3,000m in search of squid.

LOOKING AROUND

This beluga is raising its head above the water to look around. This is common behaviour because belugas are inquisitive creatures. This is a mature animal, pure white in colour. It has quite a short head with a rounded melon. Unusually for whales, the beluga has a noticeable neck, allowing it to turn its head. It also has a wide range of facial expressions and often appears to be smiling.

beluga whale

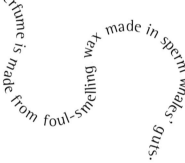

COW AND CALF
This sperm whale cow is swimming with her calf. Cows suckle their young for at least two years, staying in a nursery group with other cows and calves. This picture shows the unique body shape of the sperm whale, with its huge blunt snout. The sperm whale does not have a dorsal fin, just a triangular lump on its back.

sperm whales

HIGH SOCIETY
This pod of belugas is swimming in Arctic waters off the coast of Canada. Belugas are usually found together in such pods, because they are very social animals. Note the typical body characteristics, including broad stubby flippers and the lack of a dorsal fin.

beluga whales

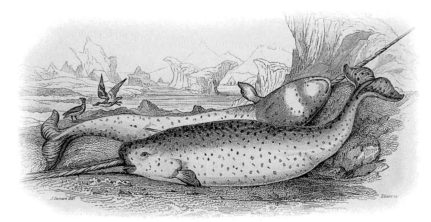

LONG IN THE TOOTH
In freezing Arctic waters a male narwhal comes to the surface to blow, its long tusk raised. The tusk has a spiral shape and can be up to 3m long. It is one of the narwhal's two teeth. A small number of males produce twin tusks.

tusk

narwhal

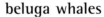

COLOUR, SHAPE AND WEIGHT
The narwhal's stocky body is much like that of the beluga, the main difference being in the colour. Whereas the beluga is white, the narwhal is mostly a mottled dark and light grey. The narwhal and beluga are almost identical in size and body shape, growing up to about 5m long and weighing up to 1,500kg.

BEAKED, PILOT AND KILLER WHALES

The beaked whales are named after the beak they have, which is rather like that of many kinds of dolphin. They are much bigger than dolphins and, unlike dolphins, they have hardly any teeth. Most have just two teeth near the front of the lower jaw. Beaked whales are found mainly in the deep ocean, far from land, and little is known about the way they live. Pilot and killer whales, however, are much better known. They are in fact part of the dolphin family and are, like many dolphins, sociable animals that tend to live in quite large groups. Because pilot whales and killer whales are mostly black, they are often called blackfish. The killer whale is the largest and best known of the family and is one of the fiercest predators in the ocean. It can be found worldwide, but prefers cooler waters. Most of the blackfish prefer warmer waters.

A TELLING TAIL
A killer whale lob-tails by extending its tail into the air and slapping the water with it. A killer whale's tail is black on top but mainly white underneath, with a distinct notch in the middle. Note also the pointed tips of the flukes.

killer whale

INTO THE BREACH
A killer whale leaps high into the air while breaching in Alaskan waters. The whale may twist and turn before it falls back to the surface with a resounding splash. Look at this killer whale's broad paddle-shaped flippers. The size and shape of the flippers and the dorsal fin mark this specimen as a male.

Did you know? Killer whales have never been known to attack humans in the wild.

killer whale

CRUISING PILOT

Here is a head-on view of a short-finned pilot whale. The animal has a broad, bulbous head, and is for this reason sometimes called the pothead whale. The flippers are long and sickle-shaped, and the curved dorsal fin rises from a broad base. It prefers tropical and subtropical regions. The long-finned pilot whale is very similar to the short-finned species, but with slightly longer flippers. This species is found mainly in the Southern Hemisphere in cool, as well as warm, waters.

pilot whale

melon-headed whales

WHITE LIPS

A pod of melon-headed whales are swimming closely together. This is typical behaviour for the species. One of the animals is spy-hopping, and shows its distinctive melon-shaped head. Note its white lips.

SLEEK PERFORMER

The superbly streamlined body of the killer whale is displayed to perfection as it comes out of the water while performing at Sea World in California. The picture also shows its characteristic oval white patch behind the eye, the white chin and the white patch at the side. There is a greyish saddle patch behind the tall dorsal fin.

FALSE TEETH

A false killer whale spy-hops, taking a good look at what is happening around it. It is showing a fine set of teeth. False killer whales have as many as 20 teeth in both the upper and lower jaws. The false killer does not look much like the killer whale and is much smaller. It has no white patches on its body, and its head is more slender.

false killer whale

beaked whale

LONE SWIMMER

A beaked whale swims alone. Most beaked whales spend a lot of time by themselves or with just one or two companions. They prefer deep waters, and some species rival the sperm whale when it comes to diving.

OCEANIC DOLPHINS

Dolphins are the most common of all cetaceans. They are swift swimmers that often perform leaps and other acrobatics as they travel close to the surface. They have sleek, streamlined bodies with, usually, a prominent dorsal fin. Their predominant body colour is dark grey on the back and white or pale grey on the belly. Many dolphins have contrasting stripes along the sides. About half the dolphin species have a long beak, and have as many as 250 teeth in their jaws. The other half have short beaks and fewer teeth. Dolphins can be found in most oceans, but they do not usually venture into the cold waters of far northern or far southern regions. Most species are highly sociable, some travelling together in groups of hundreds.

Did you know? There are about 32 species of dolphin.

southern right whale-dolphins

STRIKING STRIPES

The distinctive black and white striped bodies tell us that these two animals are southern right whale-dolphins. The back is jet black, while the beak, forehead, belly and flippers are white. Note that this species has no dorsal fin.

PORPOISING DOLPHINS

This group of common dolphins is porpoising – taking long, low leaps out of the water. These dolphins have a prominent beak and yellow or tan-coloured markings on their sides, leading from the eye. Behind the dorsal fin, the markings become grey. The dark skin on the upper back looks rather like a saddle. This is why it is sometimes called the saddleback dolphin.

Did you know? Dolphins make loud noises when hunting to panic fish into bunching together.

common dolphins

GREAT LEAPERS

These two bottlenose dolphins are launching themselves with great energy several metres into the air. Their bodies are mainly grey in colour, darker on the back and paler on the underside. The head of the bottlenose dolphin is more rounded than that of most other beaked dolphins.

bottlenose dolphins

Risso's dolphins

BLUNT HEADS

A group of Risso's dolphins is easy to recognize by their blunt heads and tall dorsal fins. Their bodies are mainly grey on the back and sides, paler on the underside. The colour becomes paler with age, and some old adults are nearly all white. The older animals are nearly always heavily scarred.

PALE FACE

This close-up shows one of the oddest looking of the dolphin species, the Irrawaddy dolphin. It has a rounded head and a distinct neck, rather like the beluga, with which it is sometimes classified. Its flippers are large and curved. It is found in rivers and estuaries, as well as coastal waters from south of India as far as northern Australia.

DOLPHIN RESCUE

An old Greek tale tells of a famed poet and musician named Arion. After a concert tour, sailors on the ship that was taking him home set out to kill him for his money. They granted his request to sing a final song. Then he jumped overboard. He did not drown because a dolphin, attracted by his beautiful song, carried him to the shore.

Irrawaddy dolphin

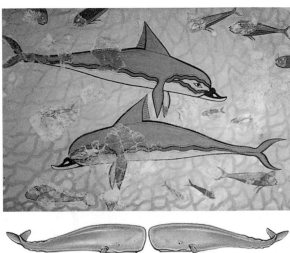

53 Oceanic Dolphins

PORPOISES AND RIVER DOLPHINS

At first sight porpoises look rather like dolphins, yet they form a separate cetacean family. They are smaller than most dolphins and do not have a typical dolphin beak. Their teeth are different too, being spade-like instead of cone-shaped. Most porpoises are shy creatures that stay well away from boats. The rare river dolphins also form a separate family. They have a long slender beak and a rounded forehead. Their flexible neck allows them to turn their head, unlike the oceanic dolphins. In the muddy waters where they mostly live, they use echo-location rather than their poor eyesight to find the fish, shrimps and other creatures they feed on. All these dolphins are river dwellers, except the La Plata dolphin, which lives in coastal waters near the La Plata estuary in South America.

Amazon river dolphin

BEAKED BOTO
The Amazon river dolphin, or boto, has the typical long beak of the river dolphins. It also has a pronounced melon on its head, which can change shape. Its body colour can vary from pale bluish-grey, as here, to pink. It has no proper dorsal fin, just a fleshy ridge along its back.

RESTING PORPOISE
A Dall's porpoise rests on the surface of the water, displaying the body features of its species. It has a stocky black body, with a large white patch on the sides and belly. The upper part of its dorsal fin and the trailing edges of its tail flukes are white as well. Unlike most other porpoises, which are quite shy, the Dall's porpoise loves to bow-ride fast boats.

Dall's porpoise

RARE SNEEZER
A Yangtze river dolphin, or baiji, thrusts its head out of the water. Like all river dolphins, it has tiny eyes and very poor eyesight. Its blowhole is circular and its blow sounds a bit like a sneeze! This dolphin is one of the rarest of all whales and dolphins, with a population that may be as small as 150 individuals.

Did you know? The harbour porpoise is rarely seen in harbours.

Yangtze river dolphin

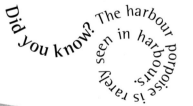

FAST AND FURIOUS

Dall's porpoises are the most energetic of the porpoises. Their swimming is fast and furious. They kick up fountains of spray as they thrust themselves through the surface of the water. Unlike other porpoises, they often swim with moving boats.

Dall's porpoises

NOISY SNORTER

The harbour porpoise is usually seen from a distance, and seldom comes near boats. It is noted for its noisy, snorting blow. The general body colour is dark grey on the back with paler patches on the flanks. Its belly is white, and it has black flippers and lips.

harbour porpoise

porpoise

Did you know? Dall's porpoises are one of the fastest marine mammals – travelling up to 35 knots.

DOLPHIN OR PORPOISE?

Porpoises are close relatives of dolphins and may easily be mistaken for them. However, they belong to a different family and have different body features. For example, dolphins have a beak, while porpoises do not. We know relatively little about porpoises as they are very shy creatures. Scientists can take advantage of strandings such as this one to study them.

polar bear

FELLOW TRAVELLERS

Whales are not the only mammals that are at home in water. Other aquatic mammals include otters and many species of seal. The otter spends most time on land and has the furry coat of a typical land mammal. Seals are much better adapted to life in the water, with a sleek, streamlined body and flippers instead of legs. They have some fur, but it is the thick layer of fatty blubber under the skin that keeps them warm in the water. Blubber is a very good insulator and stops body heat escaping. It also insulates against the cold air, when seals return to land to breed. Other mammals that are at home in the water are the dugong and the manatee. Often called sea cows, these creatures have a bulky seal-like body. They are found in rivers and coastal waters in tropical and subtropical regions.

BEAR AT SEA
The polar bear spends most of its time drifting on the pack ice in the Arctic Ocean. It often takes to the water to hunt the seals it feeds on. Instead of the whales' layer of blubber, the polar bear has a thick furry coat to give it protection from the Arctic climate. Here, temperatures can fall to -50°C and below.

Californian sea lion

FIN-FOOTED
The Californian sea lion is one of the most graceful swimmers. It swims using powerful strokes of its front flippers. Its body is much more adapted to the water than an otter's, with its paddle-like flippers. Its body is partly hairy, but is partly smooth and streamlined.

Did you know? Whales were probably descended from a 4-legged land mammal called a mesonychid.

FURRY SWIMMER
The otter spends most of its time in the water, but is equally at home on land. Its body is that of a land mammal, being four legged and furry. However, it is also adapted for life in the water. The otter's legs are short, and its toes are webbed, which make efficient paddles. Its body is streamlined, and its fur waterproof.

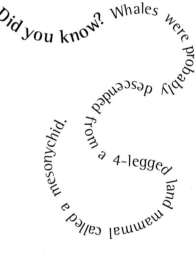

otter

whale shark

WHALE-LIKE

This creature is called a whale shark. However, it is not a whale, but the biggest fish of all – a harmless member of the shark family. It lives in warm seas throughout the world. The whale shark is huge, measuring more than 15m long when fully grown and weighing many tonnes. It feeds on plankton, which it takes in through its gaping mouth. Then it sieves out the plankton from the water through a special gill structure.

Did you know? The largest whale shark ever caught weighed 15 tonnes.

dugong

SEA COW

A dugong swims in the Pacific Ocean, just off Australia. Unlike the seals, which leave the water to breed on land, dugongs spend all their time in the sea. They have no hind limbs, but a tail, similar to that of a whale. The alternative name for the creature – sea cow – is a good one because the animal feeds on sea grasses.

walrus

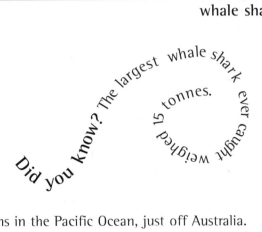

WHALE-HORSE

With its whiskers and long tusks, the walrus (whose name means whale-horse) is unmistakable. It is a large mammal of the seal family. Like the true seals, it has no external ears and it swims by means of its rear flippers. It feeds mainly on the seabed, using its whiskers to locate buried clams and its armoured snout to grub them out. The walrus excavates clams that are buried deep in the mud by squirting a high pressure jet of water from its mouth into the clam's burrow.

WHALE SLAUGHTER

The baleen whales and sperm whale are so big that they have no natural predators, although killer whales may occasionally attack them. Until a few hundred years ago, the oceans teemed with hundreds of thousands of them. Humans had hunted them for centuries, but did not take enough to affect whale populations. Then in the 15th and 16th centuries, whaling grew into a huge industry and whale slaughter began on a large scale. Whales were killed mainly for their blubber, which could be rendered down into oils for candles and lamps. The industry further expanded following the invention of an explosive harpoon gun in the 1860s. By the 1930s, whale factory ships working in the Antarctic were taking up to nearly 50,000 whales a year. In 1988, commercial whaling was banned.

WHALE SOAP
The sperm whale was once the prime target for whalers because of the large amounts of oil it contained in its massive head. This tablet of soap was made from a waxy substance, called spermaceti, from the whale's forehead.

DEADLY STRUGGLE
Whalers row out from a big ship to harpoon a whale in the early 1800s. It was a dangerous occupation in those days because the dying whales could easily smash the small boats to pieces.

Did you know? Whale blubber was made into lipstick and other sorts of make-up.

FIN WHALING
A modern whaler finishes cutting up a fin whale. A few whales are still caught legally for scientific purposes, but their meat ends up on the table in some countries. The fin whale used to be a favourite target for whalers because of its huge size. Among whales, only the blue whale is bigger.

PILOT MASSACRE

Every year in the Faroe Islands of the North Atlantic, people round up and kill whole pods of pilot whales. It is a traditional practice, which conservationists have been unable to stop. As the slaughter takes place, the sea turns red with the blood of the dying mammals.

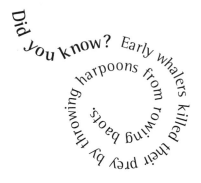

Did you know? Early whalers killed their prey by throwing harpoons from rowing boats.

KILLER NET

This striped dolphin died when it was caught in a drift net. Because it could not untangle itself, it was unable to rise to the surface to breathe, and so it drowned. Many tens of thousands of dolphins suffer the same fate each year because hundreds of kilometres of nets are cast into the oceans.

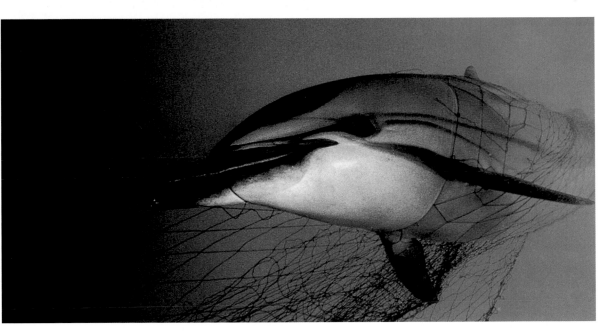

striped dolphin

Did you know? In the 1800s baleen was used to make umbrellas.

'WHALE TALE'

Moby Dick is an adventure story that was written by Herman Melville in 1851. The one-legged Captain Ahab searches for a great white whale (a sperm whale) called Moby Dick. Eventually he harpoons Moby Dick, but he and all but one of his crew lose their lives.

THE SPERMACETI WHALE

WHALE CONSERVATION

If full-scale whaling had continued to the present day, there is no doubt that many of the great whales would now be extinct or close to extinction. Even today, only a few thousand blue whales, right whales and bowhead whales remain. Because they are slow breeders, it will take a long time for their numbers to recover. Some of the other whales, such as the grey and the humpback, appear to be recovering well. These two whales are favourites among whale-watchers because they are so approachable. Whale-watching has become increasingly popular and has made people more aware of what remarkable creatures whales are and why they must be protected. Dolphins and killer whales can also be seen performing in aquariums, although the benefits of keeping these creatures in captivity are not certain.

DECLINE OF THE WHALE POPULATION

POPULATION IN THOUSANDS

200
50
48
46
44
42
40
38
36
34
32
30
28
26
24
22
20
18
16
14
12
10
8
6
4
2

blue whale   bowhead   California grey

estimated original population

present population

grey whale

GREY GREETING
A grey whale rises to the surface near a tourist boat off the Pacific coast of Mexico. It is winter, and the greys have migrated to these breeding grounds from the far north. Because these animals stay close to the shore, they are easy to reach by boat.

Did you know? The first whale sanctuary was set up in 1945.

WHALE RECOVERY
This chart shows the effect of whaling on three types of whales. By the middle of this century, the blue, bowhead and grey were close to extinction. Then whaling of these species was banned. Now populations have started to recover.

HUMPBACK SPECTACULAR
A humpback whale gives a demonstration of breaching to whale-watchers. It has hurled its 30-tonne bulk into the air, belly up, and will soon crash back to the surface in a shower of spray. Out of all the behaviour whale-watchers come to see, this is by far the most spectacular.

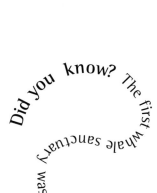

FRIENDLY FLIPPER

When most people think of dolphins, they usually have in mind the bottlenose dolphin, pictured here. One dolphin character, called Flipper, (played by several different dolphins), starred in a series of television programmes and films. These helped to focus attention on how intelligent these mammals are and how vulnerable they are in the modern world.

Did you know? You can adopt your own whale by contacting your own local whale and dolphin society.

bottlenose dolphin

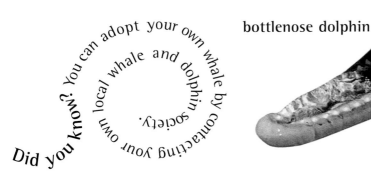

WHALE-WATCHING

A boatload of whale-watchers sees the tail flukes of a humpback whale disappear as the animal starts to dive. The boat is cruising off the New England coast of the United States where some populations of humpbacks feed during the summer months.

whale-watching off the New England coast

PERFORMING KILLER

A killer whale leaps high out of the water at a dolphinarium, drawing applause from the huge crowd watching. It is doing what comes naturally, but at the command of its trainer instead. In the wild, the killer whale is a deadly predator, but in captivity – with all meals provided – it proves docile and friendly.

killer whale

Did you know? Despite an international ban on whaling, some countries continue to hunt whales.

GLOSSARY

A

Antarctic
The region around the South Pole and Southern Ocean, including the continent of Antarctica.

Arctic
The region around the North Pole.

B

baleen
A tough and flexible material, which forms comb-like plates in the upper jaw of baleen whales.

baleen whale
A whale that has baleen plates in its mouth instead of teeth.

beak
The protruding jaws of a whale or dolphin.

blow
The cloud of moist air that is blown from a whale's blowhole when it breathes out.

blowhole
The nostril of a whale. Baleen whales have two blowholes, toothed whales have one.

blubber
The layer of fatty tissue beneath the skin of a whale that acts as insulation against cold water.

bow-riding
Swimming on the bow wave in front of a moving boat.

breaching
Leaping out of the water and falling back with a great splash.

bull
A male whale.

C

calf
A baby whale.

cetacean
A whale, dolphin or porpoise, all of which belong to the animal order Cetacea.

cow
A female whale.

crustacean
A creature with a hard body that lives in the sea. Shrimp and krill are crustaceans.

D

dolphin
A small, toothed whale that has cone-shaped teeth.

dorsal fin
The usually triangular fin on the back of a whale's body.

E

echo-location
The method toothed whales use to find their prey. They send out pulses of high-pitched sounds and listen for the echoes produced when the pulses are reflected by objects in their path.

extinction
When a species of living thing dies out.

F

flipper
A whale's paddle-like forelimbs.

flukes
The tail of a whale.

fluking
Raising the flukes into the air before diving.

K

krill
Tiny crustaceans that are the main food for many of the baleen whales.

L

lob-tailing
Raising the tail into the air and then slapping it down on the surface of the water.

M

mammal
An animal that has warm blood and breathes air. Female mammals feed their offspring on milk from their mammary glands.

mating
When a male and female unite to reproduce.

melon
The rounded forehead of a toothed whale. It is thought to help direct the sounds the animal uses for echo-location.

migration
The regular journey taken by some animals from one region to another and back at different times of the year.

P

pectoral fin
An alternative name for flipper.

plankton
Tiny sea creatures and plants. They form the basic foodstuff for all life in the oceans.

pod
A group of whales.

polar region
The area around the North or South Pole, where it is very cold.

porpoise
A small toothed whale with spade-shaped teeth.

porpoising
Leaping in and out of the water while swimming fast.

predator
An animal that hunts other animals (prey) for its food.

pregnant
When a female animal has a baby developing in her womb.

prey
Animals that are hunted for food by others (predators).

R

rorqual
A baleen whale with grooves in its throat. The grooves allow the throat to expand when the animal is taking in water when it is feeding.

S

school
Another name for a group of whales.

species
A particular kind of animal. All animals of the same species look alike and can reproduce with one another.

splashguard
A raised area in front of the blowholes of some whales. It helps prevent water entering the blowholes when the whales breathe.

spout
Spout is another word for blow.

spy-hopping
Poking the head out of the water so that the eyes are above the surface.

stranding
Coming out of the water on to the shore and becoming stuck, or stranded.

streamlined
Shaped to slip through the water easily without much resistance.

T

tail fin
Another name for a whale's flukes.

temperate
A climate in which the weather is not too hot and not too cold.

toothed whale
A whale that has teeth and not baleen plates in its mouth. Toothed whales include sperm whales, dolphins and porpoises.

tropical
The climate in the Tropics, the region on either side of the Equator, where the seas are always warm.

W

whale
A cetacean. Commonly the term is applied to the large whales, such as the baleen and sperm whales.

whalebone
A popular name for baleen, but baleen is not bone.

whaling
Hunting whales for their meat and blubber.

INDEX

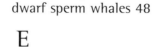